Original title:
Green Hearts, Open Windows

Copyright © 2025 Creative Arts Management OÜ
All rights reserved.

Author: Gideon Shaw
ISBN HARDBACK: 978-1-80581-762-8
ISBN PAPERBACK: 978-1-80581-289-0
ISBN EBOOK: 978-1-80581-762-8

Embracing the Symphony of Seasons

Birds in shades of lime, they sing,
Over rooftops, on a spring fling.
A squirrel dances, all in a whirl,
Chasing his tail, giving it a twirl.

The flowers giggle, in coats of dew,
Tickling the breeze, a laughter anew.
The sun wears shades, oh what a sight,
As clouds do a jig, with pure delight.

Chubby raindrops, like jellybeans,
Splash from umbrellas, the bright marines.
Kids splash and cheer, with puddle leaps,
While parents sigh, counting their sweeps.

In autumn's glow, the leaves roll away,
Mom's pumpkin pie had its own ballet.
While squirrels stash snacks, in a grand spree,
Planning for winters, oh how they'll eat!

Snowflakes waltz, on a chilly night,
Carrots and scarves make snowmen quite bright.
As laughter echoes through frosty fun,
Every season's a laugh, until it's done.

Sunlight Dances on Sill

Sunbeams prance on my window,
Tickling dust bunnies like so,
They whisper secrets of the day,
While my coffee has gone cold, I say!

The cat chases shadows nearby,
Her pounce is a sight to defy,
With each leap, she trips on air,
A ballet of chaos, beyond compare!

Blossoms in the Gentle Air

Petals tumble from the trees,
A floral shower, oh what tease!
My allergies rise with a sneeze,
But I can't help laughing, if you please!

The bees buzz in a wild parade,
They're ready for their sweet crusade,
One takes a break on my nose,
I giggle as he strikes a pose!

The Embrace of Nature's Breath

Inhale deeply, scents abound,
The grass is tickling, oh what a sound!
A wind that chuckles, how it plays,
Messing up hair in fantastic ways!

The trees converse, gossiping leaves,
While squirrels plot, rolling their sleeves,
A funny dance of roots below,
As laughter sways with every flow!

Chasing Light Through Tender Gaps

Fingers of sunlight stretch and sway,
Sneaking through curtains to play,
They find me sleeping with a snort,
And send me running for a sport!

I chase those rays, like a kid,
Forgetful of all things I did,
In my room where shadows loom,
I'm the jester in my own bloom!

Gentle Touch of Nature's Breath

A leaf slipped by, with quite the flair,
It tickled my nose, I jumped in mid-air.
The breeze has jokes, it dances around,
Whispering secrets, without a sound.

The flowers giggle, they sway and tease,
As pollen plays tag with a buzzing bee.
A squirrel threw acorns, what a surprise,
I laughed as they fell, from branches that rise.

Fields of Joy Beyond the Threshold

Past the door where daisies sprawl,
I saw a rabbit trip and fall.
He shrugged it off, with such a grace,
Then zoomed away, a wild race.

A butterfly snickered, off it flew,
Wings like a clown suit, painted in hue.
I chased it on, with a silly grin,
Hopping along, let the fun begin.

Nature's Call from Sunlit Spaces

In the sunlit patch, ants held a ball,
They laughed and cheered, but I missed the call.
Tumbling over each other, what a sight,
They played until dusk, oh what pure delight.

A snake slid by, with a smile so sly,
"Are you joining us?" I heard it cry.
I waved and thanked it, with a big grin,
But all I could do was watch the fun spin.

The Color of Endless Horizons

The clouds wore socks, mismatched for fun,
While raindrops tapped, like they'd just begun.
A rainbow appeared, and laughter was loud,
Nature's own joker, delighted the crowd.

The sun gave a wink as it settled low,
Even the shadows began to glow.
As twilight whispered tales of the day,
We danced with the stars, in a goofy ballet.

Fables of Sunlit Spaces

In a field where the daisies play,
A cow danced hip-hop, bright as day.
The sun wore shades, quite the sight,
Sipping lemonade, feeling light.

Bees in bow ties buzzed with flair,
While ants hosted a picnic fair.
A rabbit rapped with a carrot mic,
As clouds cheered on, 'what a hike!'

Charmed by the Wild's Embrace

A squirrel wore a tiny hat,
While pondering where his acorns sat.
The trees whispered gossip with glee,
About the raccoon's latest spree.

Frogs had a band, croaking in tune,
Under a crescent whimsical moon.
A fox danced tango, all in a spin,
While the owl cheered, 'Let's begin!'

Invitations from the Heart of Spring

A snail on roller skates rolled by,
Challenging the daffodils up high.
The wind played tag with the butterflies,
While laughter echoed, filling the skies.

A ladybug planned a fancy feast,
For bugs of all sorts, quite the beast!
With crumbs of cake and drops of tea,
Everyone sang, 'Come dance with me!'

Dappled Sunlight on Wandering Souls

A cat in shades, tail held high,
Stole a sunbeam, oh my, oh my!
The wind tickled feathers, made them dance,
As flowers giggled, 'What a chance!'

A turtle sprinted, well, as much as he could,
While a butterfly promised he'd look good.
With artful swirls and whimsical sighs,
Nature giggled under bright, open skies.

Glimmers of Hope on the Horizon

In a garden of socks and mismatched shoes,
The sun wears shades, as the daisies refuse.
Worms throw a party, they dance in the dirt,
While ants play a game of who'll get to the dessert.

The clouds are all chuckling, so fluffy and bright,
They play hide and seek with the stars in the night.
Butterflies gossip about their flashy attire,
While crickets compose tunes, setting hearts on fire.

Through the Grille of Dreams

Peeking through portals where shadows convene,
A squirrel named Gary dreams big of cuisine.
He plans a feast, with acorns galore,
But ends up with sandwiches, spread on the floor.

The raccoons arrive, all dressed up the same,
They strut through the garden, it's quite the acclaim.
With masks on their faces, they raid the buffet,
And laugh through the chaos, come join the display.

A Tapestry of Nature's Whispers

Under the tulips, a gnome takes a nap,
While hedgehogs discuss their best ways to trap,
The sunbeams are playful, they tickle the leaves,
And tease the ants' worries, like mischief, it weaves.

A banana slug slides by, in his vibrant suit,
Declaring himself the next fashion recruit.
Everyone giggles, as he struts to impress,
With sparkles and glitter, what a fine mess!

Revelations in the Canopy

Tree branches are making a giggling pact,
They bounce with the breeze, it's a giddy act.
Owls hoot in rhythm, they've started a band,
While fireflies twinkle, all over the land.

Under the moon, the foxes take flight,
On unicycles spinning, what a funny sight!
With tails like confetti, they jump and they play,
In the world of weirdness, they cheer on their way.

Rays of Hope in Every Cranny

In the cracks of the pavement, life finds a way,
A sprout dressed in sequins, ready to sway.
It wiggles and giggles, a sight most absurd,
Even the ants start to dance, undeterred.

Sunlight tickles the edges of puddles below,
A frog croaks a tune in a peppy, green bow.
The clouds share a laugh as they float on by,
They've seen it all, oh my! And they can't deny.

The Gentle Stir of New Life

A dandelion sneezes, sending wishes afar,
It dreams of adventures, riding the wind's car.
Butterflies chuckle, with colors ablaze,
They flit and they flutter, in whimsical plays.

A worm gives a wink, in the garden's embrace,
Offering secrets in a wriggly race.
"Grab your tiny shovel, dig a little right here,
What treasures await? Well, let's make it clear!"

Dreams Within a Leafy Realm

In the thicket of chatter, the leaves have a ball,
Gossiping softly, throwing shade for us all.
"Did you hear about the squirrel? Oh, the scandalous thief,
Stealing acorns and hearts, oh what a belief!"

Mice wear tiny glasses, plotting their schemes,
Building a kingdom made from wild, wacky dreams.
The moon overhears, giving a giggly cheer,
"Let's toast with some dew, what a party right here!"

Warmth in the Shade of Old Trees

Under the branches, where shadows ensue,
A gathering of critters, in a lively tableau.
The raccoon reads fortunes, flipping old leaves,
While the owl nods off, oh, who would believe?

"Pinch me," whispers a snail, "is it really this grand?
The fruit flies are DJing, it's all so well planned!"
With laughter and joy, the vibe's set to chill,
In the realm of the trees, there's always more thrill.

Reflections of Serenity's Glimpse

In the park, a duck dared dance,
Wobbling funny, his little prance.
Squirrels giggled from up on high,
Thinking they could touch the sky.

Sunbeams tickled the summer ground,
As butterflies spun round and round.
A napkin flew, oh what a sight,
It twirled like a kite, oh so bright.

Chasing Light Through Fragrant Gardens

Bumblebees buzz, an awkward cheer,
Humming their tunes with no sense of fear.
A garden gnome wearing shades so cool,
Stands proudly, like he's ruling the school.

Flowers whisper secrets as I stroll,
Their petals tickle, but that's the goal.
A dandelion sneezed, what a show,
Seeds taking flight, like they're off to go!

Hues of Emotion in Open Air

Rain clouds rolled in, a mischievous crew,
Then dumped a splash of paint, wild and new.
Puddles became perfect mirrors to fame,
Reflecting laughter as if it were a game.

Children sailed boats made of tin foil,
While parents scrambled, all in toil.
A dog jumped in, with such a flourish,
Who knew mud could be so nourish?

Flourishing Thoughts by Morning Light

Morning coffee, oh what a mess,
Spilled by a cat who thinks it's a fest.
Birds on branches hold a concert so bright,
Singing out tunes and stealing the light.

Sunflowers watch in wide-eyed surprise,
As a snail zooms past in a grand disguise.
A butterfly better luck with its flight,
Lands on my toe, oh what a delight!

Canopies of Hope

Under umbrellas of leafy surprise,
Squirrels plan their acorn heist with tiny eyes.
A bird drops a worm, oh what a feat,
The garden's a stage for nature's sweet treat.

Laughter erupts as the wind goes wild,
Tickling the trees like a playful child.
The daisies nod, they've got the right moves,
While bumblebees dance in their silly grooves.

A rabbit sips tea from a porcelain cup,
Wears a monocle, gives a prim little up.
The flowers gossip, saying he's quite the catch,
But he's just a fellow who's lost in his batch.

In this sanctuary, giggles bloom bright,
Under a ceiling of leafy daylight.
Comedies grow under twinkling sunbeams,
Spreading joy like the silliest dreams.

Secrets Beneath Sunlit Vines

Twisted tendrils whisper with glee,
As moonlit secrets peek from every tree.
Rabbits yawn wide, hidden in the shade,
While the flowers plot their next parade.

Jellybeans rain down on a sunny hill,
Where ants march proudly, they're never still.
A ladybug boasts of her daring flight,
But trips on a petal and laughs at her plight.

Underneath arches of emerald delight,
Chirping crickets compose songs at night.
They chirp tales of frogs in tuxedos so sleek,
And fireflies flicker, the glow is quite chic.

In this green circus, where oddballs convene,
Every nook has its charm, it's quite a scene.
Where laughter is found in the smallest of things,
And nature itself seems to wear funny wings.

Fresh Views from Loved Nooks

Hammocks swing gently in the summer air,
Sunny spots offer a comfy affair.
A cat naps with dreams of mice on parade,
While sunflowers giggle, their blooms never fade.

Comfy chairs with cushions of bright checks,
With bugs telling stories, amidst squeaks and pecks.
A squirrel on a branch shares the latest scoop,
While daisies bounce in a cheerful loop.

Teacups spin wildly in a cozy corner,
A mouse pens his memoir, a clever warner.
The chairs hold the secrets of stories told,
Of adventures and mishaps—the brave and the bold.

From these cherished nooks, laughter takes flight,
Every moment blooms, a joyful delight.
So gather your friends, let the fun reconnect,
In this whimsical world, with smiles to collect.

Earthy Reflections in Windowpanes

Through the glass, a frog leaps high with flair,
While shadows of butterflies dance in the air.
The garden's alive with a raucous cheer,
As dopey old gnomes sip their cups of beer.

A lizard lounges, sporting shades like a star,
Feasting on sunlight, dreaming of afar.
The wheelbarrow's full of giggles and grime,
It's the playground of dreams, timeless as rhyme.

Outside, the daisies are ranting of weeds,
While sunbeams trickle like forgotten creeds.
The windows reflect the quirks of the yard,
Where mischief and laughter are never too far.

With every glance, nature throws a jest,
In this world of charm, we find our best rest.
So peek through the panes, let the fun begin,
As life's simple joys spark laughter within.

A Gateway to Flourishing Dreams

In a garden that dances with glee,
A chicken debates with a bumblebee.
They argue all day, who's wiser, who's bold,
While a snail just laughs at being too slow.

Sunflowers waltz in the gentle sun,
A cat on the fence crochets just for fun.
The trees wear hats made of floppy leaves,
And the worms plot mischief while folks just believe.

The Poetry of Nature's Glance

A squirrel recites from a tiny book,
As butterflies take a sneak peek and look.
Each line is a giggle, each stanza a cheer,
Nature's shy sonnets bring laughter here.

The daisies gossip in vibrant hues,
While dandelions flaunt their shiny shoes.
A frog croaks a ballad, oh so off-key,
Creating a ruckus with perfect glee.

Embraces Found in the Fresh Air

The sunshine tickles the backs of my knees,
As ants in a meeting argue 'who's cheese?'.
A ladybug teaches a dance to a snail,
The crowd gathers 'round, hearing each tale.

Clouds float by, giving high-fives with flair,
While raccoons are plotting to find a new chair.
A picnic is brewing with laughter and cheer,
And the breeze joins in, whispering, "Stay near!"

Each Breeze Holds a Story

The wind carries whispers from faraway lands,
While kittens conspire with playful hands.
A story unfolds in a tumbleweed's roll,
As rabbits debate who will steal the show.

The trees share secrets in rustling tones,
Excited young sprouts squeak out their groans.
A breeze tickles all, from bushes to pines,
And the sun throws a party with candy and twines!

A Symphony of Fresh Beginnings

In a garden of giggles, seeds we will sow,
Tangled in weeds, watch their fumbles and flow.
Sunbeams are tickling, the daisies all cheer,
Gardening's easy, if you just hold your beer.

Unruly tomatoes play hide and seek,
Whispering secrets; I can barely speak.
The radishes blush, in their veggie parade,
While worms dance the cha-cha; oh what a charade!

Cucumbers twist like contortionist dreams,
While shadows on lawns plot their mischievous schemes.
The scarecrow's a dandy, with style and a grin,
As birds throw confetti while plotting to win.

So join in the laughter, let worries all fade,
Life's quirky surprises are meant to upgrade.
With every odd harvest, and giggle we share,
We dream up our lives with joy in the air.

Laughter Echoes in the Meadow

In a meadow of mirth, flowers tell jokes,
Bees bust out dances, like happy folks.
A butterfly winks, with a twist of its wing,
As crickets provide an evening of swing.

The sun's making faces, a spontaneous yawn,
While rabbits hop high, oh how they fawn.
Squirrels throw parties, they drink from the stream,
While caterpillars plot their next grander scheme.

A hiccuping frog starts a ribbiting beat,
While ants form a conga, all quick on their feet.
Daisies roll laughter, as daisies can do,
As mushrooms make puns, and the sky's painted blue.

With giggles as currency, we pay for our day,
Laugh lines emerge, as the clouds float away.
For every tall tale that the meadow might tell,
It's laughter we cherish, we know it's quite swell.

Fragrant Dreams in Bloom

In the garden of aromas, scents frolic and twist,
Where thyme tells a tale and sage isn't missed.
The mint giggles softly as the basil grins wide,
While lilacs hum songs, a fragrant joyride.

An onion speaks wisdom, its layers unfold,
While garlic defends, with a story so bold.
Petunias whisper secrets, sweetly to thyme,
As daisies throw shade, in a dance so sublime.

A daffodil jokes with a sunflower fair,
While the wind starts to tickle, it messes my hair.
The soil's a storyteller, dirtier than sin,
And petals parade happily, looking for win.

So let's toast our bouquets with a glass of fine dew,
Let laughter be our fertilizer, hearty and true.
For in fragrant adventures, we bloom with delight,
As we spin all our dreams in colors so bright.

Revelations at Dawn

A rooster crows loudly, but forgot his own rhyme,
As sleepy-eyed flowers wake up just in time.
The sun slips on slippers, all cozy and warm,
While coffee beans giggle, embracing the charm.

Mist dances like spirits o'er fields rich with glee,
While rabbits play tag, quite unbothered by tea.
The dawn chuckles softly, as shadows retreat,
And crickets throw parties to celebrate sweet.

The morning dew winks, with a sparkle or two,
As squirrels spin tales of the mischief they knew.
With giggles of petals, and chatter of trees,
Nature's own laughter floats softly on the breeze.

So embrace all the hubbub; it's nature's fine play,
Tomorrow's a chance for another bright day.
With joy in our pockets and wonder in sight,
We dance with the dawn, till the stars kiss the night.

Nature's Canvas Unveiled

In every leaf, a secret grin,
A dance of colors starts to spin.
The squirrels wear hats, quite absurd,
While bees recite their buzzing word.

A flower whispers, 'Look at me!'
While ants hold court with bold decree.
The sunbeams play a game of tag,
As butterflies in laughter brag.

The willow waves, a funny friend,
Telling tales that never end.
The clouds roll by, a fluffy tease,
They bounce in joy upon the breeze.

Oh, nature's art, so whimsically,
An endless draft of jubilee.
With every bloom and giggling breeze,
We find ourselves, quite humor-free.

The Silence of Mossy Nooks

In cozy corners, critters hide,
With cheeky grins, they wait inside.
The moss speaks softly, 'Shh, not a peep!'
While beetles plot and schemers sleep.

A toad on a log begins to croak,
A frog jumps up to make a joke.
The snail slides by in slow parade,
While shadows giggle in the glade.

Mossy stretches—what a sight!
The shrooms play poker every night.
In silence, life's oddities trot,
Amidst the weeds, oh, what a lot!

So if you stumble on this show,
Remember all the laughs they sow.
In every nook, a story sways,
With playful jests, in leafy ways.

Emblems of Renewal at Twilight

As twilight fades, the crickets chirp,
The moonlight winks with a gentle burp.
The daisies laugh and twist their stems,
While shadows compete in silly whims.

A raccoon juggles acorns by chance,
While fireflies join in a glow-in-glance.
The stars begin their sparkly chat,
Grinning down at a sleepy bat.

Renewal's here, a nightly spree,
The bushes wave, as if to flee.
With every wink, the world seems bright,
A comedy under starry light.

So gather 'round this twilight show,
Let laughter blossom, row by row.
In nature's script, we find the rhyme,
Where funny moments steal the time.

Petals at the Threshold

Petals tumble at the door,
Each color laughing, wanting more.
The roses wink with fragrant flair,
While daisies dance without a care.

A breeze flutters, a slapping sound,
As laughter echoes all around.
The tulips nod with cheeky grins,
While violets plot their little sins.

At every step, a carpet bright,
As blooms rejoice in pure delight.
Nature's jesters, bold and free,
In petals laughing silently.

So open up, embrace the cheer,
For every little bloom holds dear,
A world of humor, fresh and fun,
Where petals dance 'til day is done.

Tranquil Scenes Unfolding Outside

Birds are plotting in a tree,
Chasing squirrels with glee.
A cat spies with narrowed eyes,
Wondering who'd win the prize.

The sun spills tea on the lawn,
As ants march like it's dawn.
A breeze tickles the flower's nose,
And the tulips strike a pose.

Clouds giggle, puffs of fluff,
While butterflies act all tough.
The daisies dance, oh what a sight,
As the bugs prepare for flight!

In this garden of goofy charms,
Life's a comedy of warm arms.
Nature's humor never tires,
Even when it misfires.

Lattice of Life Interwoven with Sunbeams

Sunbeams doodle on the floor,
While the wind knocks at the door.
A spider weaves a laugh or two,
Creating webs of morning dew.

The plants gossip, ever sly,
"Did you see that bird fly by?"
A snail debates its slow-paced race,
While the daisies giggle in place.

The shadows play hide and seek,
With each tick, they begin to squeak.
Laughter ripples through the park,
As the sun begins to spark.

At dusk, the stars will poke their heads,
Pointing out all the funny threads.
In this weave of life and fun,
A tapestry that's never done.

Breath of Fresh Perspectives

A breeze whispers silly jokes,
As flowers giggle, blooming folks.
Trees sway their branches wide,
Inviting laughter in their stride.

The bees throw a buzzing parade,
While the sun blinks, unafraid.
Grasshoppers hop with glee and flair,
Creating tunes that fill the air.

The pond plays a reflective game,
With fish making faces just the same.
Ripples dance on water's skin,
While frogs practice their silly grin.

In this world of playful sights,
Every corner brings delights.
Nature's muse never tires,
Always sparking fun-filled fires.

Nature's Invitation to Wander

The path beckons with a grin,
"Come and chase the breeze within!"
A squirrel stops, strikes a pose,
While a butterfly shares its woes.

Pebbles roll with a cheeky laugh,
Telling tales as they craft.
Trees stand tall in a silly dance,
Waving branches at every chance.

The hills chuckle with every step,
Tickling toes, oh what a prep!
Clouds stroll by in playful rows,
A silly show that never slows.

As laughter trails through every bend,
Nature's warmth feels like a friend.
With every turn, a surprise awaits,
Life's whimsies open all the gates.

Frames of Abundance and Love

In a frame of bright colors, I found a sweet shoe,
Made for a gnome who's got a green thumb too.
They dance with the daisies, in a comical style,
Trips and tumbles make the garden worthwhile.

With buckets of sunshine, they water the beans,
Creations of laughter where craziness reigns.
A scarecrow in pajamas, struts down the lane,
Fashion-forward, he's the king of the grain.

Squirrels in tuxedos, what a fancy affair,
Balancing on branches, without a care.
They sip on acorns while gossiping sprout,
Whispers of secrets that no one's found out.

When morning erupts like a joyous parade,
And the garden gremlins aren't one bit afraid.
It's a wild jamboree, where love blooms with cheer,
In the frames of abundance, where joy is sincere.

Echoes of Growth Behind Glass.

Behind the glass, the plants wave hello,
As if they're rehearsing for a wacky show.
The ferns in tuxedos, the daisies with flair,
Each leaf like a joke—laughter fills the air.

The sunflowers giggle in sunshine's embrace,
Winking at bumblebees zooming apace.
Through tickles of breezes and whispers of glee,
The echoes of growth hum a jubilant spree.

Vines tangled like earphones, a hilarious sight,
They reminisce tales of a wild, funny night.
The tomatoes are blushing, oh what a tease,
They strut on their branches, just aiming to please.

The moon on the window, a silly old chap,
Watches the seedlings set up for a nap.
With dreams sprinkled lightly like dew on a lawn,
Each laugh of the garden greets the dawn.

Breezes Through Unfurling Leaves

Breezes fly by, playing tag with the trees,
Leaves giggle softly, swaying with ease.
The cedar's cracked jokes, oh what a delight,
As whispers of humor grow louder at night.

In the dance of the petals, the daisies all cheer,
For the wind's funny pranks, oh how they endear.
While tulips applaud with their colorful caps,
They lean on each other, collapsing in raps.

Laughter erupts from the shrubs, quite insane,
As squirrels take selfies in a whimsical vein.
"Look at my paws!" says one, striking a pose,
While butterflies giggle at the silliness grows.

Through breezes that twist and turn like a kite,
The leaves look around, aglow in the light.
In this comical world where nature can play,
Each moment's a joke, in its funny ballet.

Whispered Secrets of the Garden

Beneath the whispers of the leafy brigade,
Floral jesters tell tales, all carefully laid.
With a chuckle or two, they plot out their fun,
As followers of humor mingle in the sun.

The carrots hold meetings with the peas in a knot,
Discussing the latest on the bugs they have fought.
Sneaky radishes join, spilling secrets so kind,
Sharing one-liners that brighten the mind.

The roses all gossip about their sweet scent,
While the basil argues, "I'm better, just bent!"
Tulips sport crowns, laughing loud with glee,
"I'm the queen of this patch, just wait and see!"

As shadows then twinkle with the twilight's embrace,
The garden erupts in a light-hearted race.
With whispered secrets that tickle and tease,
Nature's own comedy, filled with sweet ease.

Nature's Open Invitation

Nature called, I think it's mad,
Inviting squirrels, a little chad.
The flowers giggle, the trees just sway,
As I trip on roots and lose my way.

A bird lands cheeky on my nose,
With chirps and tweets, it playfully glows.
I swear that branch just wiggled too,
Or was it just my lunch that blew?

Rustling Leaves of Fond Memory

Leaves are chatting, what do they share?
"Remember that time we flew through the air!"
"Oh yes!" said a twig, "We caused a stir,
When we landed in soup, what a funny blur!"

Acorns rolling, playing hide and seek,
While I trip over roots, oh how they tease!
"Who needs butter?" they giggle with glee,
When falling on pancakes, just let it be!

Shadows of Sunshine and Blossoms

Sunshine throws shadows, they dance in delight,
While daisies wink at the bees taking flight.
"Who's got the nectar?" they buzz and they hum,
As I chase my hat while the laughter's from mum.

A daffodil sneezes, pollen in the air,
While the branches above just shrug and stare.
"Be careful!" they whisper, "Don't spill that drink,"
But I trip on the grass and just start to sink.

From Openings Unto Infinity

Windows ajar, the breezes conspire,
Whisking away all my plans, oh the fire!
"Catch that sandwich!" I shout in despair,
As a gust takes my hopes and chuckles with flair.

The clouds are flipping pancakes, it's true,
While sunbeams juggle, it's quite the zoo.
"Open wide," call the petals, join in the fun,
As I slip on the grass and giggle, I run!

Fragments of a Sunlit Reverie

A cat perched high on the sill,
Dreaming of fish with a curious thrill.
Sunbeams dance on a floor of crumbs,
While squirrels debate if it's lunch or funs.

The dog's tail wags like a blur of paint,
Chasing shadows, making pranks quite quaint.
Butterflies flutter with a gentle giggle,
As the cat plots a chase, ready to wiggle.

A vase shakes as the wind bleeds air,
Sending flowers flying everywhere.
The neighbors laugh at the playful tease,
A sunlit party, no need to appease.

Through the glass, quirks of life unfold,
Whispers of laughter not easily sold.
In this space where silliness runs wild,
Even the grumpiest are easily beguiled.

Sentinels of Time and Blossom

A clock with its hands on a merry dance,
Mocks the gardener in his sleepy trance.
"Tick-tock," it says, "what's the rush today?"
As daisies giggle in a sunlit ballet.

A gnome in the yard wears a crooked smile,
Eyes twinkling with mischief all the while.
He plots and he plans to create some fright,
Bouncing at night with the stars shining bright.

Wind chimes chime in a whimsical tone,
Announcing to all that they're never alone.
Birds drop by for an impromptu soirée,
Avec a dash of drama, and a sliver of play.

In this garden where chaos seeds roar,
Each breath whispers, "What's outside the door?"
A world of laughter, where time takes its cue,
Sending echoes of joy in a vibrant view.

Melodies of the Wind's Dance

The breeze brings secrets from places unknown,
Tickling my hair, and chilling the groan.
Leaves rustle softly, spinning their tale,
Riding the whispers like ships on a gale.

A squirrel debates on a quest for a nut,
While a nearby flower gives a cheeky strut.
A rabbit hops as if leading a race,
Trying to keep up with the wind's wild pace.

The butterflies argue on colors to wear,
"Pink or blue?" they cry in the sunlit air.
With fluttering wings, they break into song,
Making the flowers sway along all day long.

Oh, what a circus! The garden's the stage,
With laughter and dance, breaking every cage.
Cheerful chaos, each day brings a grin,
Celebrating life, where the fun can begin!

Serenity at the Window's Edge

From the window, a parade unfolds,
With pigeons in tuxedos on daily strolls.
A ladybug lands with a hint of sass,
As the world below rushes by in a mass.

Sunflowers gossip about bees and nests,
Parrots squawk tales, putting all to the test.
"Did you hear?" chirps one with a glint in her eye,
As honeybees buzz with a purpose to fly.

Postmen chime with letters to share,
Whispers and giggles float through the air.
At times, a leaf dances through the lane,
Creating a scene of delightful refrain.

Life through the window, a comedy fair,
Bathed in the glow, every worry laid bare.
With laughter and light, we greet each new day,
In this quirky theater where humor leads the way.

Dreams Laid Bare on the Lawn

Socks off, I run on the grass,
Chasing clouds, what a silly class.
The sun's my judge, with laughter to share,
Dancing in circles without a care.

Mice in the bushes now gossip away,
While I concoct plans for a picnic ballet.
Picking wildflowers, my crown will be bright,
But ants steal my honors, they nibble with bite.

The lemonade's warm but the laughter is cold,
Neighbors peek out; let the stories unfold.
With dandelions plucked by the root,
I crown myself king, what a loony hoot!

Bubbles fly high like dreams in the air,
As I stumble and slide without any care.
Frogs in their chorus applaud every flop,
In this wild, whimsical, lawn-tastic shop!

Warmth of Yesterday's Blossoms

In a teacup, my dreams brew tea,
But the cat thinks it's meant for he.
With petals that brighten old memories,
I dodge sneezes while buzzing with bees.

Yesterday's blossoms, a fragrant delight,
But pollen attacks with such sneaky bite.
I flail and I dance like a quirky old fool,
As violets giggle, the garden's own school.

A butterfly laughs at my not-so-deft sway,
"Try yoga!" it whispers, then flits away.
With leaves as my audience, I put on a show,
But down goes my hat, in the wind it will blow!

The glow of the sun enhances my charm,
While ants form a line, intent to disarm.
Just watch, I'll take flight on this silliness spree,
For warmth is the laughter, and joy is the key!

Life Outside the Frame

Framing my world through a fussy old lens,
I peer out the window; the cat makes amends.
Squirrels debate how to raid the bird feast,
While I'm stuck here inside, not a wild enough beast.

Picture perfect moments, they flit in and out,
But my tripod's a tripod, or so I would tout.
With every new angle, I slip and I slide,
Life's going outside while I'm stuck here inside.

Flowers posing, birds taking a nap,
I snap at the memories, but lose the whole map.
"Chase after that sunbeam!" the garden will shout,
As I adjust my focus, the laughter just pouts.

In frames made of vines, I catch each odd glance,
But a breeze steals my hat; oh, another missed chance!
Outside's the grand show, while I stand in my dome,
In the art of silliness, I always feel home!

Joy Spilling Over the Lattice

Through a tangled lattice, laughter will creep,
With buckets of joy, I'm too full to keep.
The wind chimes sing a tune of delight,
While I role-play the roles of a jester, not quite.

Cups overflow, tea turns to a geyser,
As jokes blossom wild, I'm the garden's advisor.
Witty remarks with a side of sweet breeze,
I dance with the petals, a butterfly tease.

Laughter leaks out like a wildflower sprout,
I juggle my giggles; what's this all about?
The fence might just tip with my raucous cheer,
While bees hold their meeting; they hum in my ear.

So here in this garden, the joy spills in clumps,
With humor and breezes, I tumble in jumps.
Lattice of laughter, build bridges with glee,
In the carnival dance, we're all wild and free!

Sunbeams Between the Vines

In the garden, a pickle dances,
Sunlight winks, oh what are the chances?
Tomatoes giggle, their laughter free,
As cucumbers plot a wild spree.

The shadows play tag, it's quite absurd,
While grasshoppers chirp, oh haven't you heard?
A scarecrow waltzes with a floppy hat,
Who knew the farm could throw such a spat?

With every breeze, the daisies jig,
And bees buzz by, they do a little gig.
A ladybug twirls, a glittery show,
Chasing down ants like a dance-off pro.

So weave through the vines, don't lose your shoes,
In this patch of joy, you just can't lose!
Grab a sunbeam, and let laughter fly,
Because in this garden, we reach for the sky.

The Voice of the Wind's Caress

I heard the wind whisper, 'Why so glum?'
A squirrel replied, 'I lost my drum!'
The trees shook their leaves in fits of glee,
While the clouds puffed up like they were free.

A feather floated down, all soft and light,
And shouted, 'Come on, let's dance tonight!'
A kite got jealous and flew up high,
But it tangled itself and had to cry.

The whispers grew louder, caught on a breeze,
'Hey, moody cloud, can we rattle some trees?'
Down below, tiny flowers took a stand,
Waving their petals, forming a band.

So if you hear whispers when you're alone,
Join the wind's laughter, don't mope or groan!
For even the breeze knows how to amuse,
With tumbles and giggles, there's nothing to lose.

Savoring the Morning Hues

Oh, breakfast time, what a curious sight,
Pancakes are flipping, almost in flight!
A toast calls 'Cheers!' from the counter so wide,
As coffee grins proudly, black as a slide.

Eggs dance in their pan, doing the flip,
While orange juice twirls on a citrus trip.
"Banana, you're slipping!" the toast makes a jest,
"Stay steady, my friend, you're the ultimate zest!"

The buttered toast shimmies on its plate,
'This morning's a party, let's celebrate!'
But oatmeal, feeling left out, starts to pout,
Until the milk says, "Let's cream it out!"

So all gather 'round for a feast so bright,
With laughter and flavors, pure morning delight.
Grab your forks and let joy be the rule,
Savor the hues, life's a whimsical school!

Echoes of Life Beyond Glass

Inside the room, there's a curious sound,
A goldfish sings while spinning 'round!
The curtain sways, a ghost in disguise,
Shouting, "Open the windows, let's reach for the skies!"

Outside, a cat plots an escape,
While a bird tweets loudly, a feathered drape.
"Oh, to be free!" the poor fish laments,
While the window displays a parade of events.

Children run past, their laughter flies high,
While a ticklish breeze teases by.
The goldfish grins as it hears all the fun,
Imagining adventures under the sun.

With a flip of its tail, it proclaims with grace,
"Life's better together, no need for a space!"
So let's laugh together, whether in or out,
For the joy of the day is what life's all about!

Verdant Whispers

A leaf sneezed loud, the trees took fright,
Squirrels giggled, what a sight!
Grass tickled toes, oh what a tease,
Nature's laughter floats on the breeze.

Rabbits hop with a hoppy cheer,
Playing tag, their tails appear.
A chubby worm wriggles with glee,
"Come join the fun! It's wild and free!"

Bumblebees dance, a buzzing song,
"Don't step on me! I'm all day long!"
Flowers flirt in colorful hues,
"Pick me! Pick me! You can't refuse!"

So swirl in joy, let worries flee,
In vibrant rooms of nature's spree.
With every grin the world becomes,
A funny place where laughter drums.

Breezes Through Canvas

A gentle gasp through paint-stained air,
Brushes wiggle without a care.
A canvas giggles, splashes of fun,
While colors collide, the joy's begun.

The sky made of jelly, oh what a shock!
A rainbow trampoline, flip-flopping rock.
Each stroke a chuckle, canvas grins wide,
With whimsical worlds where dreams collide.

Puddles of joy, little raindrops fall,
Dancing on rooftops, having a ball.
I paint my worries, let laughter emerge,
In this windy laugh, I feel the surge.

So flutter about through the brush and breeze,
Let colors tickle your heart with ease.
For life is a palette, a dance divine,
With each stroke we cherish, our spirits shine!

Ecstasy of Emerald Leaves

Leaves in a whirl, a giggly spree,
Swirling round in joyful glee.
A hiccup from branches, a comedic twist,
Nature's own stand-up, magic on mist.

Frogs in tuxedos, croaking the tunes,
The pond's a stage beneath the moons.
Each leap a joke, each splash a laugh,
In frothy waters, they take a bath.

The clover smirks, a treasure to find,
Winking at luck, playful and kind.
Dandelions fly, wishes take flight,
Sprinkling joy in the soft twilight.

So dance with the leaves, twirl with delight,
In a world that sparkles, so wonderfully bright.
With every chuckle, may spirits revive,
In nature's embrace, we're fully alive!

Heartstrings in the Meadow

In the meadow, a symphony plays,
With butterflies boogying through sunny rays.
The daisies chuckle, their petals sway,
While ants march in lines for a picnic buffet.

A witty rooster sings tunes so bright,
Poking fun at clouds with all his might.
Crickets chorus a hoppy rhyme,
As grasshoppers groove, dancing in time.

Bumblebees juggling pollen with glee,
Nature's own circus, come and see!
The sun beams down with a cheeky grin,
As laughter erupts, the fun begins.

So leap through the meadow, embrace the play,
For joy's a reminder in games each day.
Each chuckle a thread, connecting us tight,
In fields full of laughter, everything's right!

Sunlight's Embrace on Soft Pages

A cat naps deep on a sunny sheet,
Chasing dreams of a fishy treat.
The dog wears shades, looking quite cool,
While ants play chess beside the pool.

A squirrel in socks raids the pantry,
Dancing around like a little canty.
The goldfish giggles with a bubbly cheer,
As the parrot squawks, 'There's no way out of here!'

Gnomes on the shelf are planning a coup,
While the houseplants whisper, 'What shall we do?'
A ladybug winks, feeling quite grand,
As petals boast of their colorful stand.

When sunshine tickles the pages of books,
Stories take flight on silvery hooks.
With laughter so loud from pages turned,
In this cozy nook, our hearts have burned.

An Invitation to Nature's Symphony

The frogs are croaking, a late-night band,
Creating a concert unwritten and grand.
Fireflies twirl like tiny fairballs,
While crickets play tunes at nature's walls.

The raccoons party with snacks they bring,
While a hedgehog tries to learn how to sing.
A tree with arms lifts its branches high,
'This is the spot where dreams can fly!'

A butterfly flirts, wearing polka dots,
While beetles play cards in their favorite spots.
The moon rolls in, like a sleepy friend,
As night unfolds, and fun won't end.

In this symphony of chirps and squeaks,
A melody blooms, each note it seeks.
With laughter and light, the night takes flight,
As the woodland speaks until the sunlight.

Lush Dreams on Sill and Sky

A window swings wide, with a cheerful grin,
Welcoming dreams that swirl and spin.
The clouds play peek-a-boo with the sun,
While daisies cheer, 'Oh, what fun!'

The flowers gossip, sharing their thoughts,
While a thirsty bee steals sweet swots.
Mice on a tiny bicycle zoom,
While grass blades join in to blossom and bloom.

A pot of basil wears a big hat,
Saying 'I'm ready for tea with the cat!'
With laughter echoing from balcony heights,
As the basil prances under starry lights.

Between the sill and the endless blue,
Nature spins tales that feel so true.
With fun in the air and laughter so high,
These lush little dreams soar up to the sky.

The Dance of Unseen Breezes

An unseen breeze pulls on my hair,
Twirling whispers mingling with air.
It tickles my nose, oh what a tease,
While the trees giggle and dance with ease.

A squirrel in motion, a wobbly twirl,
He's trying to impress a sweet acorn girl.
The flowers sway in clumsy delight,
As shadows play tag in the fading light.

The wind paints stories across the grass,
While butterflies flutter, daring to pass.
With a howl of joy, the zephyr sneers,
Turning our laughter into musical cheers.

In this dance of smiles and chuckles galore,
Life spins around, who could want more?
With unseen breezes that twirl and sway,
Every moment's a chance to laugh and play.

Caresses of Unseen Breaths

In the park, my hat took flight,
Chased by a squirrel, what a sight!
It danced around, played peek-a-boo,
While I stood still, feeling quite blue.

The breeze tickled my nose, oh dear,
As leaves laughed loudly, could they hear?
A gust swirled round like a sneaky thief,
Leaving me plagued with confusion and grief.

A dandelion whispered, "You're not alone!"
As pollen tickled my funny bone.
I sneezed so loud, the birds took flight,
A comedy show, what a delight!

And in the end, with a giggle I trod,
Feeling like nature's own little clod.
With sunshine smiling, I took a quick spin,
Thanking the wind for the chuckles within.

Radiance in the Silhouette of Leaves

A shadow giggled, casting shade,
While I danced around, unafraid.
Branches swayed like they knew the song,
Inviting me to join, and I tag along.

Sunbeams peeked through the rustling crowd,
Creating a spotlight, oh so loud!
The leaves whispered secrets of times gone by,
While I waved hello to a passing pie.

A butterfly landed, a true fashionista,
Wings flipping like they're a wild fiesta.
I tried to impress, with a clumsy twirl,
But tripped on my own feet, what a whirl!

Yet, in the laughter of trees and air,
In this silly life, I found flair.
With smiles aplenty dancing in the shade,
Nature's bright jesters had it made!

Whispers of Life Beyond Touch

A breeze crept in, a playful fluke,
It teased my hair like a friendly spook.
"Catch me if you can!" it laughed and flew,
I chased it down, my energy too.

Grass tickled my toes, a giggly bed,
As flowers nodded, plans in their head.
A wild daisy winked, "Join the fun!"
But my toe caught a root, oh what a run!

The wind chuckled low, a mischievous breeze,
Whispering jokes amongst the trees.
Each leaf shared a punchline, bold and slick,
Leaving me dizzied, and wanting to stick.

As dusk set in, with laughter and glee,
I waved goodbye to my plant buddies.
They waved back with petals, a silly display,
Life's jokes abound in the light of the day!

The Artistry of a Breezy Day

The sky dressed up in a quilt of blue,
With clouds as puffs, a fluffy crew.
A rogue breeze tickled my lunch in flight,
Sailing my sandwich, what a fright!

I grabbed at the air, like a clown on stage,
Searching for crumbs, oh what a rage!
The ants laughed hard, their picnic in sight,
While I juggled napkins, what a delight!

A chipmunk chattered, "Look at the fool!"
As I tried to outsmart wind with a rule.
"Be still!" I shouted, waving my hands,
But the wind just giggled, shifting its plans.

So, I embraced the chaos, and danced a bit,
Laughing with nature, never to quit.
On this breezy canvas, we painted the day,
With crumbs in the air, life's hilarious display!

Serenity Amidst Urban Rhythms

In the city buzz, a cat takes a nap,
While pigeons plot their next pizza flap.
Taxi horns honk like a jazz band at play,
A squirrel steals crumbs, then scuttles away.

Office folk rush, lost in their grind,
Yet someone in traffic is dancing, unwind.
A tall guy in shorts and a polka-dot tie,
Struts like a peacock, oh my, oh my!

Lattes spill dreams on the subway floor,
As folks read their phones, but miss what's in store.
Laughter bursts forth like a bubbling brook,
While a dog sniffs a lamp post and gives it a look.

Among concrete giants, a flower raises its head,
A rebel against order, where chaos is bred.
With roots deep in laughter and petals of cheer,
This odd little bloom makes the skyline sincere.

Breath of Fresh Beginnings

Awake with a yawn as the sun spills its light,
A jogger salutes, in neon, quite a sight.
Morning birds chirp in a symphonic tweet,
While a mop splashes water on someone's bare feet.

Coffee aroma lingers, a bold, lively dance,
As croissants roll by in a buttery trance.
The barista spills foam on a smiley face,
And hot cocoa dreams leak into the race.

Joggers collide with a roller-skate crew,
As a child on a scooter zooms past, vroom-vroom!
Umbrellas pop open, a signature style,
And puddle-jumping kids make it all worth the while.

New winds now blow with a pancake flip,
Crisp notes of fall in each playful quip.
With laughter and joy as we start anew,
Let's dance to the rhythm of a morning view!

Chasing Shadows in Sunlight

Under the sun, a dog starts to prance,
Chasing its shadow in a wild, goofy dance.
While kids by the fountain just giggle and shriek,
An old man at a bench nods off with a squeak.

The ice cream truck jingles, a siren's delight,
From penguins in hats, what a funny sight!
They pirouette wildly, clumsily bold,
And slip on spilled sprinkles, oh, what tales told!

Chasing the breeze, a kite takes off high,
While a cat on a leash gives a bewildered sigh.
As shadows grow long, the park changes hue,
And laughter appears as a butterfly flew.

In the chase, there's magic of silliness found,
Each corner we turn brings joy all around.
With giggles and grins, we frolic till dark,
Tracing our shadows, a whimsical spark.

Nature's Kiss on Wandering Souls

A picnic awaits neath the wiggly trees,
Where ants hold a meeting with crumbs from the cheese.
A squirrel steals a grape, and zooms with a flair,
While folks on the blanket are lost in their stare.

Bicycles weave like spaghetti on wheels,
As laughter erupts over silly rubber heals.
Two ducks in a row march with purpose divine,
While a kid in a cape thinks he's saving the line!

Clouds turn to poodles, a whimsical sight,
As pizza delivery dives in for a bite.
The wind hums a tune, a playful serenade,
And flowers start waltzing, a colorful parade.

In the embrace of joy, we wander so free,
With tickling blades of grass, oh such glee!
Nature wraps her arms, with laughter and cheer,
As we dance to her beat, year after year.

Soulful Respite at Daybreak

A squirrel dances on a wire,
As dawn spills light like spilled cider.
Birds in bow ties give a cheer,
They know it's time for morning beer.

A cat in shades surveys the scene,
While worms throw parties, lean and mean.
The toast pops up, a golden surprise,
While butter waits, but still denies.

The garden gnomes play poker too,
With acorns stacked as chips, who knew?
The flowers laugh and share their tales,
Of beetles dressed in tiny veils.

The sun peeks in, nudging the grass,
To wiggle and jiggle, none shall pass.
As day breaks forth, let laughter reign,
In this quirky realm, joy is the gain.

Flickers of Life in Every Frame

A fox with glasses reads the news,
While frogs in hats drop all their blues.
The fireflies flicker with a grin,
Dancing around like they're on gin.

A raccoon in a top hat claims,
He's launched a line of fancy games.
While rabbits hop, and spin like tops,
In this wild scene, laughter never stops.

The camera clicks, a perfect shot,
Of ants on trikes, a silly plot.
Each snapshot tells a tale so grand,
In this zany world, pure fun is planned.

With every blink, a new concept rolls,
Bouncing about like wriggly trolls.
Let's capture moments that tickle the soul,
In this frame of laughter, we become whole.

Harmony in the Soft Glade

Stumbling on mushrooms dressed in flair,
The toads are juggling without a care.
Twists and turns in this vibrant space,
Where even the hedgehogs join the race.

Butterflies sing in harmony's tune,
While the sun plays peekaboo with the moon.
The daisies sway, a disco crowd,
With whispers of laughter, bustling loud.

Crickets play backup in this grand show,
As the whole glade rocks to and fro.
The wind hums sweetly, like a drunk bard,
Spinning tales that leave us charred.

This joyful glade holds secrets dear,
Beneath the laughter, lies no fear.
Come join the frolic, shake off the old,
In this magic realm, let fun unfold.

Treetops Whisper Sweet Secrets

The owls debated the best tree to climb,
While squirrels recite their best nursery rhyme.
Branches sway like they're at a ball,
Sharing the gossip, oh what a haul!

With acorn hosts in woodland attire,
The chipmunks dance beside the fire.
Laughter erupts like a popcorn pop,
In this tall party, nobody stops.

A breeze carries giggles across the skies,
As rabbits tease, donning clownish ties.
The foliage whispers, secrets in air,
Of feasts and pranks, and not a care.

With each rustle, a joke is told,
The tree leaves fearlessly break the mold.
Join in the merriment, let spirits soar,
In these treetops high, laughter's the core.

www.ingramcontent.com/pod-product-compliance
Lightning Source LLC
Chambersburg PA
CBHW072124070526
44585CB00016B/1551